Edwardian Rambles

Written and Illustrated
by Henry Atty

Alfresco Books

Copyright © Jeanette Morgan

First published in 1998 by *Alfresco Books*
7 Pineways, Appleton, Warrington, WA4 5EJ

A CIP record of this book is available from the
British Library.

ISBN 1 873727 10 0

Cover design by Jo Berriman

Lettering by Bob Porter

Printed and bound in Singapore

PREFACE

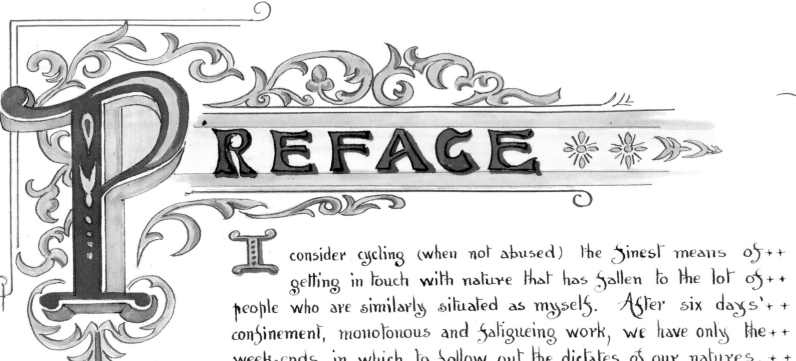

I consider cycling (when not abused) the finest means of ++ getting in touch with nature that has fallen to the lot of ++ people who are similarly situated as myself. After six days' ++ confinement, monotonous and fatigueing work, we have only the ++ week-ends in which to follow out the dictates of our natures, ++ and to those who love the country cycling gives the opportunity+ of drinking in to the full the inexhaustable beauties that +++ unfolds. I have to confess that the most enjoyable + + + rides I have had in the past have taken place on the + + + Sundays. Some people are apt to look on Sunday + + + cycling as a desecration of the Sabbath, but personally + + I take an entirely different view of it. I consider no + + +

cathedral is to be compared with nature as a fitting place in which to worship. Often when listening to a sermon in which the ~ preacher elaborates on a future life in which we are to reside in a golden city with gates of pearl, I think it would be no heaven to me to be cast amongst so much splendour, I much prefer the daisy covered field or leafy woodlands. I often ~~ think they have formed a wrong conception of life and ~~~ immortality. Most of the religious bodies look on eternal ~~ life as the special privilege of humanity. For my part I ~~ consider that all life, vegetable, animal and human are ~~ eternal. Then again I think nature preaches far better ~ sermons than we hear from the pulpit. For example the parson is always impressing on our minds the idea of living a life so that in the end we may attain eternal glory, and for this purpose a form of worship is set up so that this end may be attained, which eventually creates a ~

self-righteous, ceremonious religious fanatic. Natures' lesson is slightly different, instead of living for eternity live for the present. Look at the daisy, a small and apparently insignificant flower, but what a different aspect to the scene the daisy makes, and how incomplete the scene would be without it, and so it is with the whole of nature: the tree may stand out with greater majesty than the daisy or blade of grass, but how insignificant it would be if left on its own, showing us that though our lot may be poor and to all appearances unimportant we are all the same the component parts of a beautiful picture of human effort and enforcing on our minds the responsibility of making that life as beautiful an addition and perhaps the one touch that is needed to complete the picture. Occasionally we may be passing a rubbish heap out of which may frequently be seen a small plant struggling for existence, presenting a pretty picture in itself when compared with its unpleasant surroundings, though probably it is stunted in growth and its bloom is not to be compared with other plants of its nature who are fortunate enough to be in ground more conducive to their growth. Eventually it seems to gain the mastery over its surroundings and converts the origin of its birth into something of a ~ semblance of beauty. I always think there is a striking lesson in this, as it ~ teaches us that though our environments may be poor we may rise above them and stand out with distinctive prominence from our surroundings, ~ though, I am sorry to have to admit, that in human life as in nature it is oftener the case that we succumb to our environment. I am afraid if I go on in this strain much longer I will be giving the impression that the following outings are sermonettes, but that idea will soon be dislodged on perusing same as I intend ~ giving expression to all my thoughts and moods on each little excursion, and if I should be caught in the rain or am unable to obtain light refreshment when needed or get a puncture or breakdown on one of these excursions the sermonette idea will be completely annihilated.

H. Atty.

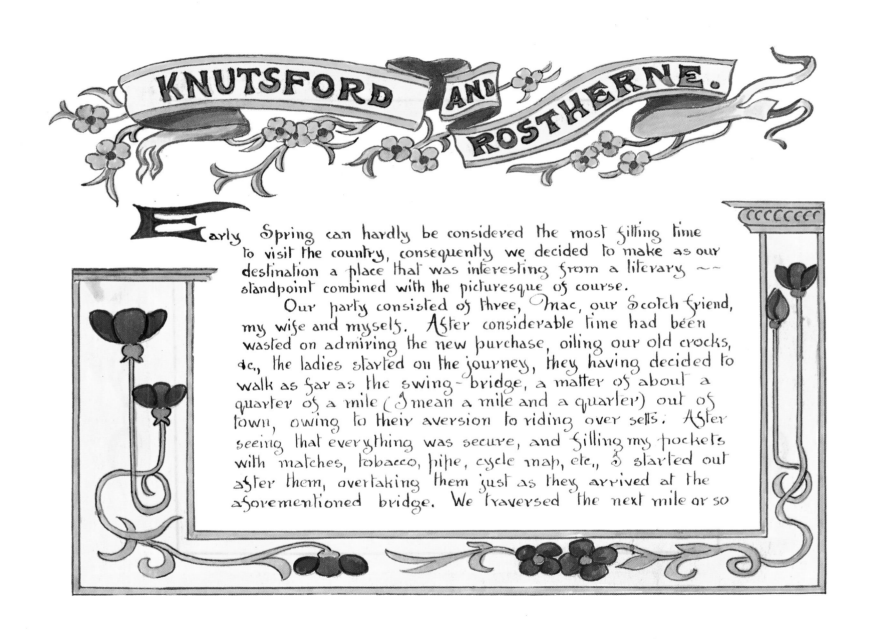

KNUTSFORD AND ROSTHERNE.

Early Spring can hardly be considered the most fitting time to visit the country, consequently we decided to make as our destination a place that was interesting from a literary ~~ standpoint combined with the picturesque of course.

Our party consisted of three, Mac, our Scotch friend, my wife and myself. After considerable time had been wasted on admiring the new purchase, oiling our old crocks, &c., the ladies started on the journey, they having decided to walk as far as the swing-bridge, a matter of about a quarter of a mile (I mean a mile and a quarter) out of town, owing to their aversion to riding over setts. After seeing that everything was secure, and filling my pockets with matches, tobacco, pipe, cycle map, etc., I started out after them, overtaking them just as they arrived at the aforementioned bridge. We traversed the next mile or so

in grand style, Mac, by the way, commenting on what a grand pastime cycling was and what an exhilarating influence it had over one, at which my wife agreed, adding the rider, "especially when going down hill." Of course Mac rejoined that she enjoyed going up-hill as much as down hill, being a gentle hint that her superior machine would take her over all the little hills we were likely to encounter on this journey, but alas she spoke too soon as we shortly arrived at a hill a quarter of a mile in length, and before reaching the top Mac was suddenly seized with a strong desire to eat an orange, of course she wasn't tired, oh dear no, simply dry, that was all, my wife was only too willing to comply with this request, but strange to say there was no mention made of the oranges when we had dis-mounted, I expect they were forgotten in Mac's anxiety for me to try her machine to see if it wanted oiling. It is a peculiar thing how the imagination grows on you that your machine wants oiling when climbing a hill. The switchback nature of Knutsford Road makes it hard for inexperienced cyclists like ourselves to make

much progress and by the time we had reached the ~ entrance gates of High Legh Hall and had been half blinded and chocked with dust from the passing motor cars, we unanimously agreed to stop at the first available place and help to lighten Mac's machine by eating an orange each. After this our progress seemed to be much better, probably owing to the road being not quite so hilly as it was from Warrington to High Legh.

~ ~o~ ~

About a mile or so out of Knutsford we rode in the midst of a band of cyclists of the usual ~ ~ shilling an hour fraternity, as per illustration on next page, which was a fine excuse for Mac to fall in the rear on the pretence that the company was not of her chosing.

~ ~o~ ~

By this time we were beginning to feel rather hungry and having brought a large pie with us we decided to eat the same at the most convenient place

we could locate within close proximity to the town, consequently on arriving at the Heath, which the authorities of Knutsford have converted into a pleasure ground, placing sundry seats here and there among the gorse bushes, we availed ourselves of the opportunity of demolishing the pie and having a little rest, before exploring the ancient town of Knutsford, which by the way derives its name from King Canute, being first known as Cunetesford, and from that to Knottesford, and eventually Knutsford. It appears Canute marched through the district in 1017 on his way to the north.

I have not given any description re scenic effects from Warrington to Knutsford as it is hardly worth describing, it being purely pastoral country, which when viewed from a macadam road, over which motor cars continually are passing, raising clouds of dust and covering the hedges with a thick layer of same, it makes it practically impossible to give a satisfactory account of the country.

☙ ❧❧❧

The first thing that struck us on entering the town was the quaint irregular streets and houses, and for a town of over 5,000 of a population it retains a freshness of a small country village. To those who have read any of Mrs. Gaskell's books it proves particularly interesting as most of the places described are still in existence, and we could almost imagine that her characters were impersonified in some of the people we see passing along its narrow thoroughfares and alleys. The whole town seems to have Mrs. Gaskell written all over it, although she is not the only person of note of which the town boasts as we read that Lord de Tabley (poet of no small repute), Edward Penny, R.A., Edward Sharp, M.A., F.R.I.B.A., were born at Knutsford, also that Lord Clive and General Wolfe were partly educated there.

We made our way along one of these narrow streets (Princess Street), till we ultimately arrived at the old church, which I believe was built in the year 1744. It was a very nice old church but in our admiration of the crocus which flourished in abundance in the church-yard and our desire to visit the grave of Mrs. Gaskell in the old Unitarian Chapel yard a little further on, we overlooked many of its architectural beauties. Our course took us past the gaol, practically a modern structure (built in 1880).

On arriving at the railway station we took a sharp turn to the left arriving ultimately at Brook Street Chapel, which was built in 1688. It is rather difficult to locate as it stands off the roadway and is almost entirely obliterated from view by a building directly in front of it. It is of a barnlike appearance with small windows, by no means

BROOK STREET CHAPEL

picturesque from an architectural stand-point, but for all that its antiquity combined with the fact that in the graveyard in which it stands the body of the late Mrs. Gaskell is interred, to an extent glorifies it. After visiting the grave and taking a small memento of our visit in the form of a leaf, we made our way along King Street to the Gaskell Memorial Tower. My wife and Mac decided to have a cup of tea at the elaborate restaurant adjoining the tower, after which they had the pleasure of viewing Knutsford from the top of the tower. While they were having tea, I went to the "Rose and Crown" adjoining the tower, which holds the proud reputation of being the oldest public-house in Knutsford, its date of erection being 1641. I must say it looked more antique from the outside than from the inside, but still I was not sorry I visited it as I carried away with me a most refreshing memory of the place. The day being yet young and we feeling fresh after our light refreshment, we decided to extend our journey through Rostherne and Lymm and consequently after viewing the Ruskin

"Rose and Crown"
Knutsford.

Institute, a peculiar structure, built on the Eastern principle, we made our way past the entrance to Satton Hall, the seat of the Earl of Egerton of Satton, and along a narrow lane skirting the park which widened and improved as we went on. The wooded nature of the park on our right, combined with the more open country on our left, the rambling hedge growth and the absence of motor traffic made it a most enjoyable run, till we eventually arrived on the highway from Altrincham to Knutsford, I hope I never have occasion to go far along this road, for oh, ye gods, talk about dust and motor cars: it was one continual stream of motor cars and it was an impossibility to judge what the landscape was like, as it took us all our time dodging cars and keeping dust out of our eyes, fortunately we had not far to go before we turned off, along a narrow winding lane to our right, which eclipsed the other for beauty, being more varied in nature. Eventually we arrived at ~ Rostherne, undoubtedly the beauty spot of the whole journey.

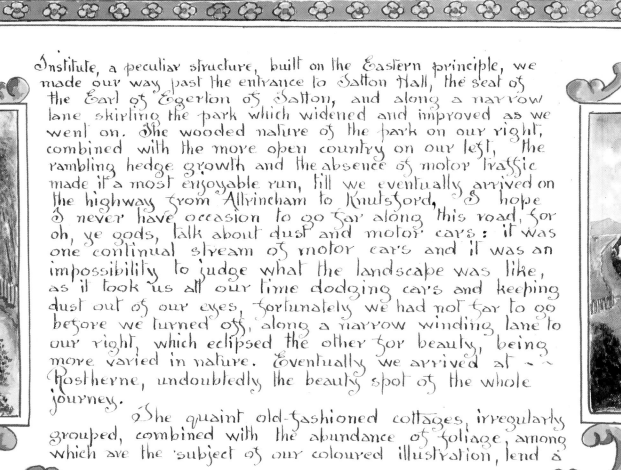

The quaint old-fashioned cottages, irregularly grouped, combined with the abundance of foliage, among which are the subject of our coloured illustration, lend a

ROSTHERNE

picture never to be forgotten, though I am sorry to say the cottages last referred to are to be razed by order of the Earl, who has taken an aversion to them. The noble earl has subjected villagers to several petty tyrannies, the most notable being the fact that he has prohibited the cottagers providing refreshments to visitors, in consequence of which enormous protest meetings we organized in which ~~ hundreds of cyclists took part, but all to no avail.

The prettiest view is to be obtained from Rostherne Church-yard. The church is pleasantly situated on a hill overlooking Rostherne Mere, the largest lake in the county, its extreme length being 1250 yards, and in places is 103 feet deep. This broad expanse of water, as seen from the church-yard, is apt to remind us of the lake district. The banks of the mere are exceptionally well wooded. The dark, sombre reflection of the trees, combined with those of the yellow rushes which grow in profusion at the water-edge, present a most pleasing and ~~ fascinating view, especially as we have in the background an ~ addition to the landscape in the form of a hill which is also not lacking in woodland, from among which we catch a glimpse of the square tower of Bowdon parish church.

Rostherne Church itself is by no means lacking in interest, it being a very old structure, the most notable feature of which being an embattled tower with pinnacles, portions of it being of great antiquity. Inside the church is a beautiful marble monument to the memory of Beatrix Egerton, who was found dead in bed at the age of 21. Over the body in a stooping position is the representation of an angel with expanded wings. On the north side of the church is an ancient stone coffin.

The narrow winding lane from Rostherne to the highway is by no means lacking in interest. First we have the school-house, woodland scenery, meadows, occasional glimpses of the mere, in fact a varying combination of all that go to make some of Cheshire's most interesting rural scenery.

We were so disgusted with our previous experience of the highway that we decided to give it the "go-by"; consequently we continued along country lanes till we ultimately arrived at the little hamlet of Millington, an ideal spot for pic-nic parties, though rather dangerous to cyclists not conversant with the road owing to its hilly nature. My wife had the misfortune to lose control of her machine, of course it was my fault for not notifying her that there was a hill, and had she been dashed to fragments at the bottom I should have been to blame. When I happened to remark that it was just a nice free-wheel they became very indignant and tried to convince me that we must have travelled at the rate of at least 50 miles an hour, and that riding from the summit of Snowdon to Llanberis was nothing compared to it, these were not actually the sentiments used, but it was something to that effect they tried to drive into my incomprehending brain. From this point to Symm is a most excellent country lane, flat and even, in fact we could not have chosen better roads from a cycling standpoint on the whole of the journey.

LYMM CHURCH AND DAM

Lymm is an ideal little village. A day can be spent to advantage in exploring the district, but on holiday times it suffers the fate of all pretty places in close proximity to large industrial centres, that of overcrowding. Lymm Dam presents a very peaceful looking picture, the church and trees and sloping nature of its banks helping to ennoble the view, but the continual passing of waggonettes, motors, cyclists and occasional roudy bands of visitors has a marring effect and is altogether out of harmony with the picture. We had intended having tea in Lymm but failed to locate a suitable place so I suggested deferring same till we reached Statham, but when we arrived there we saw so many

machines outside the cottages we intended patronizing,
and it looked as if we would have to wait a long time
before being attended to that we decided to wait
till we reached home, it only being a matter of about
3½ miles it was no great hardship, so we proceeded
along the low road, through Thelwall, passing the
Pickering Arms and Thelwall Church and ultimately arriving
at the swing bridge, Latchford, fatigued and hungry.
At this point I left the ladies to walk home, while I rode on
to prepare for tea, which was most acceptable after a
pleasant day's outing.

THELWALL

PICKERING ARMS

HOYLAKE.

After three or four weeks' collection of excursion bills, reading up of guides to holiday resorts and the studying of maps, we decided that we would take a weeks' holiday, and after calculating the expenses of the various places and also the advantages of good roads for cycling we decided on Hoylake.

So as curtail expenses we decided to cycle there (a matter of about 26 miles from Warrington) but when the day came the weather was so inclement that my wife and Mac decided to go by train to Liverpool and cross over to Birkenhead and cycle from there to Hoylake, leaving me to follow on later on my machine.

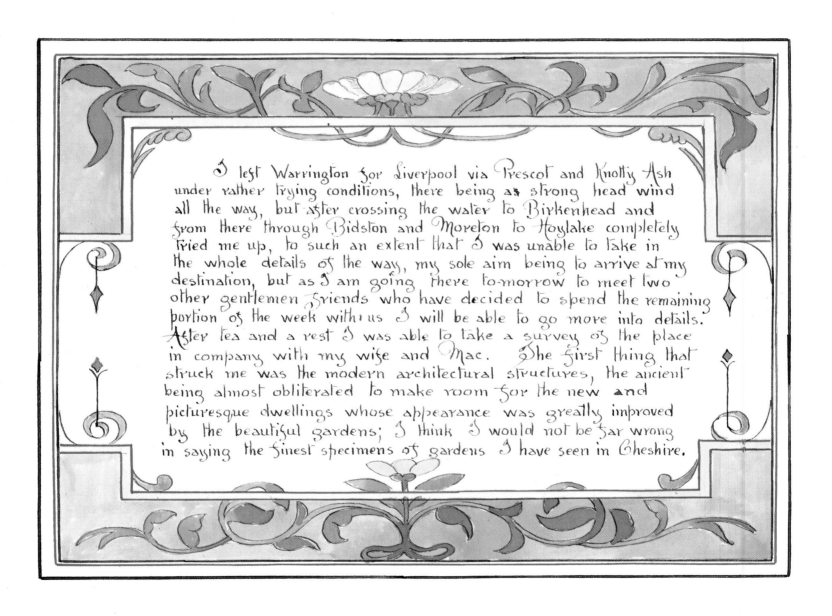

I left Warrington for Liverpool via Prescot and Knotty Ash under rather trying conditions, there being a strong head wind all the way, but after crossing the water to Birkenhead and from there through Bidston and Moreton to Hoylake completely tried me up, to such an extent that I was unable to take in the whole details of the way, my sole aim being to arrive at my destination, but as I am going there to-morrow to meet two other gentlemen friends who have decided to spend the remaining portion of the week with us I will be able to go more into details. After tea and a rest I was able to take a survey of the place in company with my wife and Mac. The first thing that struck me was the modern architectural structures, the ancient being almost obliterated to make room for the new and picturesque dwellings whose appearance was greatly improved by the beautiful gardens; I think I would not be far wrong in saying the finest specimens of gardens I have seen in Cheshire.

The "Olde Punch Bowl" Hoylake

The promenade is exceptionally fine and we had the pleasure of seeing a very pretty sunset, which, by the way is one of the main attractions of the place.

The following day being Sunday we decided to spend a very quiet day and in the morning we took a stroll as far as West Kirby, a mile and a half from Hoylake, situated on the estuary of the Dee, commanding a fine panoramic view of the Welsh mountains, the Snowdonian range lending a most attractive background, while in the foreground we have Holywell, the copper mines of Mostyn, the Point of Air and lighthouse and various farmsteads on the hill-sides. West Kirby has a little more of the antique, and also has move the appearance of a town than Hoylake. It is very pleasantly situated at the foot of the well-wooded "Grange Hill."

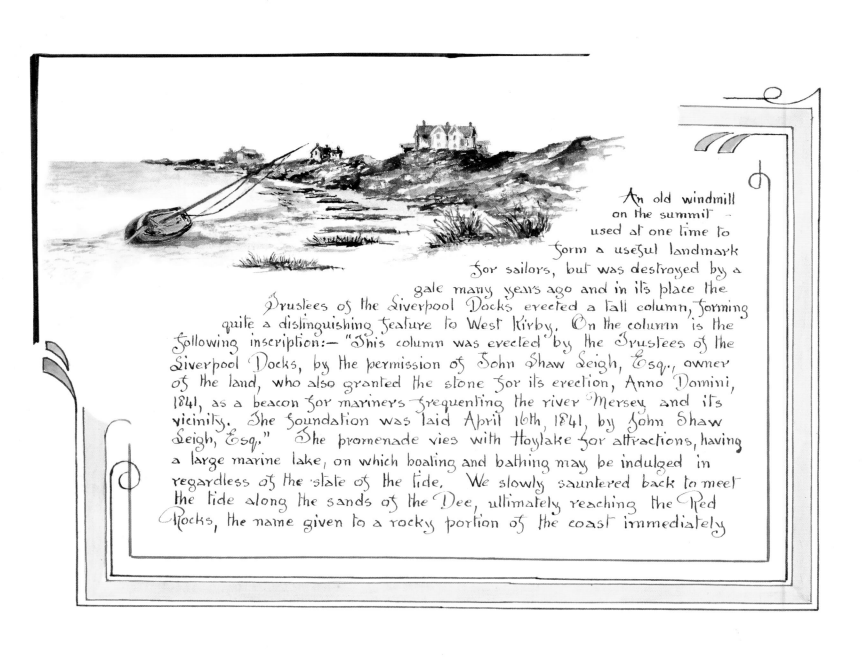

An old windmill on the summit — used at one time to form a useful landmark for sailors, but was destroyed by a gale many years ago and in its place the Trustees of the Liverpool Docks erected a tall column, forming quite a distinguishing feature to West Kirby. On the column is the following inscription:— "This column was erected by the Trustees of the Liverpool Docks, by the permission of John Shaw Leigh, Esq., owner of the land, who also granted the stone for its erection, Anno Domini, 1841, as a beacon for mariners frequenting the river Mersey and its vicinity. The foundation was laid April 16th, 1841, by John Shaw Leigh, Esq." The promenade vies with Hoylake for attractions, having a large marine lake, on which boating and bathing may be indulged in regardless of the state of the tide. We slowly sauntered back to meet the tide along the sands of the Dee, ultimately reaching the Red Rocks, the name given to a rocky portion of the coast immediately

opposite the notorious Hilbre Island, on which at one time a monastery used to stand, which was said to have been endowed by King John with the sum of 10s. a year in consideration of a light being always displayed to guide sailors. It is now used as a look-out and telegraph station by the Mersey Dock Trustees. The tide was just breaking on the rocks when we arrived there, and after drinking in the beauties of the sea and inhaling the fresh invigorating breeze we made our way via Hoylake promenade and across the sand-hills home with a fine appetite for our dinners.

In the afternoon we went out with the intention of taking a short cycle run, but rather exceeded the distance going, instead of going 10 miles or so we went at least 20 miles. Our course took us through West Kirby, ascending Grange Hill. The Beacon Hill is a conspicious object, partly covered with heather and bracken and commanding fine views of the surrounding districts. Caldy village is what particularly struck me, if such it may be called, the church nestling among the trees, the black and white reading-room and cottage at a bend of the road, an old cross on the hill-side and the generally well-wooded nature of the country lane, presenting a most pleasing combination, from here to Thurstaston hills we have an excellent little run along a country lane with a pretty hedge growth, composed principally of poppeys, On arriving at the hills (350 feet above sea level) we decided to rest for a short time, not that we were tired, but to give us an opportunity of enjoying to the full the fine panoramic view of the Dee, Hilbre Island, the Welsh mountains and Irish sea, for which purpose we climbed a large mass of rock known as Thor's stone, which is said by some to be of Druidical or Danish origin, whatever its origin may be it is undoubtedly a fine view finder and has the advantage of being prettily situated among the heather, bracken, and gorze covered hills, which in themselves present a pretty combination of color which will remain in our memories for a considerable period. After a short rest we proceeded on our journey to Heswall, but I must say I was a little disappointed as I had anticipated seeing an ancient little village. It It certainly is an ancient village as it claims the proud distinction of being mentioned in the Doomsday Book, but it is an old village with a modern appearance.

From Heswall, through Barnston and past Arrowe Park to Upton and Moreton compensated me for my disappointment in Heswall, it being a fine little spin through country lanes which bore no trace of their close proximity to their more modern surroundings, winding lanes, thatched white cottages with pretty old-fashioned gardens, shady dells and open country being the order of the day, and we arrived home full of good intentions for the Monday when our other friends were due to arrive.

Early next morning we took a stroll along the promenade (2 miles in length) with fine bowling green, tennis courts and gardens. After a survey of the gardens and a scramble over the sandhills we were in excellent form for the good breakfast that was awaiting us on our return, after which the three of us went to Birkenhead to meet our other friends, or I should say I went to Birkenhead, leaving my wife and Mac at Bidston Hill, a favourite resort of the Liverpool people. It stands 220 feet above the sea level and is

clothed in gorse, broom and heather, amongst which the famous Bidston Observatory and Lighthouse stands, and we must not forget the windmill on the summit, it being a well-known landmark, and adding greatly to the picturesque nature of the whole surroundings. The foot of the hill is exceptionally well wooded and it is the pleasure of visitors after they are tired of the summit to ramble through these woods. I made my way to Birkenhead and the three of us met my wife and Mac at the old church at Bidston, dedicated to S. Oswald, and erected in the 13th century, the tower of the church, bearing that date is all that remains of the old structure, as it was rebuilt in 1593. From here the five of us made our way to Hoylake, and after dinner my wife decided to spend a lazy afternoon on the sandhills while the rest of us arranged a short excursion to Hilbre Island, which up to the present has been the tit-bit of the time. The experience is apt to take one back to their childhood days. To commence with we had to discard shoes and stockings to enable us to cross over a mile of sands with numerous channels of water.

ENTRANCE TO CAVE, HILBRE ISLAND.

About half way across we disturbed a large number of gulls and smaller birds who were basking in the sun on a glistening strip of yellow sand. The sight was a most beautiful one, their white breasts and wings contrasting most favourably with the sand water and clouds. As we proceeded it was a common sight to see old and young of both sex displaying more of their legs than they would care for their friend in the various towns they came from to see. On arriving at the island we were surprised at the beautiful picture it presented. We had anticipated something of a bare, rocky nature and were quite unprepared for the magnificent cliffs on the south side of the island and the green sward on the top with sheep and horses grazing on it. Every now and then we came across some fresh attraction in the shape of a cave, the jutting out of some rocks which had been washed into all sorts of fantistical shapes by the constant beating of the tide, the broad expanse of water between the Point of Ayre and the island with the Welsh mountains in the back-ground, the seaweed covering the large boulders at the foot of the cliffs, the whitewashed buildings of the Mersey Dock and Harbour board, the yachts lying on the sands, while others were anchored in one of the deeper channels, all helped to enhance the view. We were so delighted with the excursion that we left it with a full determination to pay it another visit before our week was up. We were in fine form for the tea that was provided for us, after which we spent the time on the promenade watching visitors, mostly children, donkey riding, paddling, sailing boats, digging, sand castle building and bathing receiving their full share of patronage. The special feature of the evening being a most beautiful sunset.

On the following morning we decided to pay a return visit to Caldy and Thurstaston so we started out on our machines armed with a camara. The initial stages of the journey were occupied in pointing out to one another the beautiful gardens previously referred to, and after leaving West Kirby and climbing the Grange Hill, whose beauties we were better able to investigate owing to having more time to our disposal, we made our way to Caldy village, and were successful in securing an admirable photo of a most picturesque bend in the country lane, after which we proceeded through an avenue of trees and along the poppy lined lane to Thurstaston, where we scaled the rock known as Thor's stone, of which we obtained another photo though from a photographic standpoint it could hardly be compared with the one taken at Caldy. It is one of those pictures that appear to the eye as beautiful owing to the excellent color combination, heather, bracken, red sandstone and blue sky forming a very pleasing combination which only the brush of the artist and not the lens of the camara can produce. On the whole we were very pleased with our little excursion and wended our way back to Hoylake fully satisfied with ourselves, and after tea spent the evening in listening to the music and patter of a concert party at the lighthouse.

We were all up early on Wednesday morning so that we could participate in a short constitutional before breakfast on our machines from the south end of the promenade to the north end and back (just four miles). At the extreme north end, that is the Leasowe end we were favoured with an admirable view of what is known as the Submerged Forest, in which there was numerous trunks of fallen trees. In places they were covered with tidal sludge or blue clay. It appears that the remains of deer, cattle, dogs, and relics of an ancient barbarous race have been found here. From a picturesque standpoint it was nothing, what particularly claimed our attention being the summer camp on the sand hills of the poor children of Liverpool. After breakfast we decided to pay a return visit to Hilbre Island so that my wife could have the pleasure we had had, and also to give us an opportunity of taking one or two photos. The experience was practically the same as our previous visit with the exception that we got a good picture of the cave and a humerous one of my wife and Mac paddling. On our return we were rather fatigued and in consequence spent the remainder of the day in the village, on the promenade, and also a little bowling on one of the bowling greens in the gardens, to the strains of selections from various operas given by an imperfect band of the usual seaside variety. We were so enchanted with our first game of bowls, that after elaborating on the game, each one trying to impart what little knowledge they had picked up of the game, we decided on a match, married v. single. I stood down as it made one too many. The result was a walk over for the married ones, and during the breakfast the conversation was intermixed with "so-and-so's bowl was too merry" or "you didn't have enough of thumb bias on," and similar phrases they had picked up of other players. There appeared to be only one fault and I think that was the green was not quite big enough, a five-acre field would have answered the purpose better. After breakfast we decided on a run as far as New Brighton, it being such an excellent day for cycling. The first part of the journey through Moels and on to Moreton village is hardly worth detailing as there is nothing striking from a scenic or architectural standpoint. On arriving at Moreton we took a sharp turn to the left along a very uneven country lane which eventually brought us out at the Leasowe camping ground, which was separated by an embankment from the sea. It presented an uncommon picture, scores of tents, caravans and wooden huts, occupying the whole patch of land that had been reclaimed from the sea by the erection of the aforementioned embankment, reminding one of the camp towns we read of in the gold centres. We went along the embankment for a short space and then on to the sands, over which we cycled to New Brighton, but the experience was so unpleasant that we decided to abandon the sand on our return journey. Owing to the numerous ridges, wet sand and soft, floury sands, into which the tyres sank, it made our progress slow and tedious, and we we by no means sorry to see the promenade just as we turned by the "Red Noses." From my point of view I fail to see what pleasure anyone can find in spending a holiday in New Brighton, the scenery is nil, the ~~coars~~ amusements coarse, and it close proximity to Liverpool even deprive it of the appearance of a sea-side resort. On the other hand it has a fine promenade, good sands for children, and a picturesque lighthouse, and we must not forget the tower, 621 feet in height, which is pleasantly situated in extensive and well-laid out grounds; it is also a fine centre for cyclists and is convenient to Liverpool if stranded there on a wet week. With all its advantages it is a positive relief to me to get out of it. The smell of restraunts, the common and suggestive peep shows, roundabouts, ariel railways, ice cream and hoky-poky vendors, the screaching of steamers and the general crowded appearance of the place are features that I resent. The road was fairly good from New Brighton to Wallasey village, a long street with shops and houses on each side, some old and quaint and some very modern and up-to-date. From here to Leasowe was an exceptionally good road with a good open road country on the one side, and the famous market gardens on the other. Eventually we arrived at Leasowe Castle, built by Ferdinand, Earl of Derby, in 1593, and for a long time used as a sporting residence, but now turned into a residential hotel and hydropathic establishment. The grounds are beautifully laid out, and provision is made for all kinds of out-door sports of all kinds. On reaching the enbankment at Leasowe we proceeded to Hoylake over exactly the same road that we had come. I omitted to mention the discarded lighthouse at Leasowe, built on the ground on which the camping-out takes place. It is 110 feet high and commands a fine view of the estuaries of both the Mersey and the Dee. After tea the weather looked rather threatening so we spent the night in the Hoylake lighthouse concert, which proved a very wise move as it turned out a very wet evening.

Friday being the last day for our gentlemen friends we decided to spend the whole of our time in the vicinity of Hoylake. On the morning we sauntered as far as West Kirby, had a look round the town, made a few purchases, stayed a short time on the promenade watching the boating on the marine lake and then strolled back to Hoylake along the sands and past the golf links with the intention of spending the afternoon in exposing three plates we had left on sea scenes, anticipitating a rough sea owing to there being rather a stiff breeze and we turned out again with that intention, wending our way to the red rocks, which we had thought would be the best place for that purpose, but we disappointed as far as views were concerned as there was practically no tide worth photographing so we amused ourselves by striking attitudes on the rocks and at the water edge till we had ultimately used up our remaining three plates.

After tea our friends made their departure for Warrington via Birkenhead, being highly gratified with their few days holiday, leaving us to follow on Saturday, which cast rather a depressing feeling over us, especially on the Saturday morning, when after settling up with our landlady and dispatching our luggage we started for home, being favoured with fine weather. We had gone barely a couple of miles when my wife had a puncture, and we had only just got that repaired and was just about to start when there was a loud report caused by the wire on the rim of the tyre of my wife's machine breaking. After that I had a "Derby" trundling it to Moreton, arriving at the cycle repairing establishment there at 12 o'clock, only to find the owner had gone to Liverpool and would not be back till 1.30 p.m. There was nothing for it but to stop and have dinner there, after which we had to wait till almost 2 o'clock before the man returned. It took him an hour and a half to repair it, but he made an exceptionally good job of it. On arriving at Liverpool we partook of tea. We had intended stopping there a bit but the noise and bustle got on our nerves to such an extent that we made

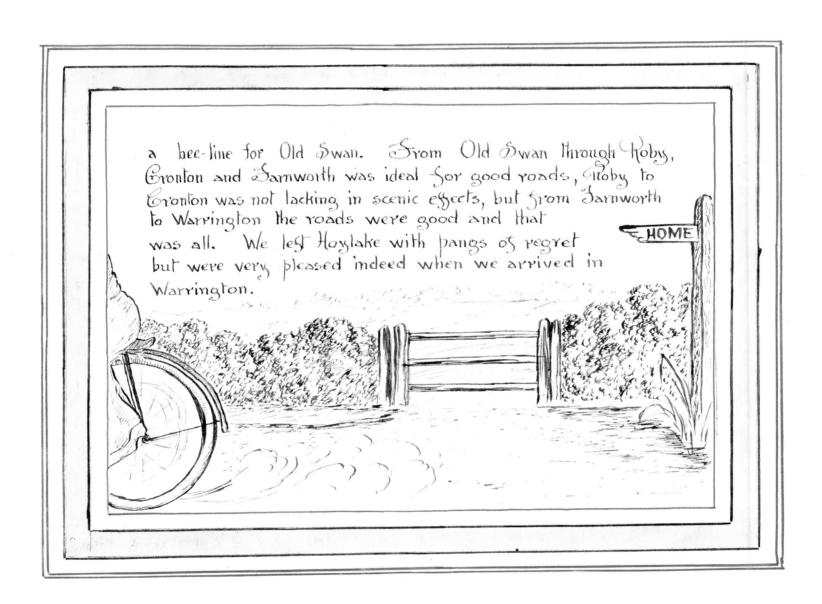

a bee-line for Old Swan. From Old Swan through Roby, Cronton and Farnworth was ideal for good roads, Roby to Cronton was not lacking in scenic effects, but from Farnworth to Warrington the roads were good and that was all. We left Hoylake with pangs of regret but were very pleased indeed when we arrived in Warrington.

HOME

Arley and Budworth.

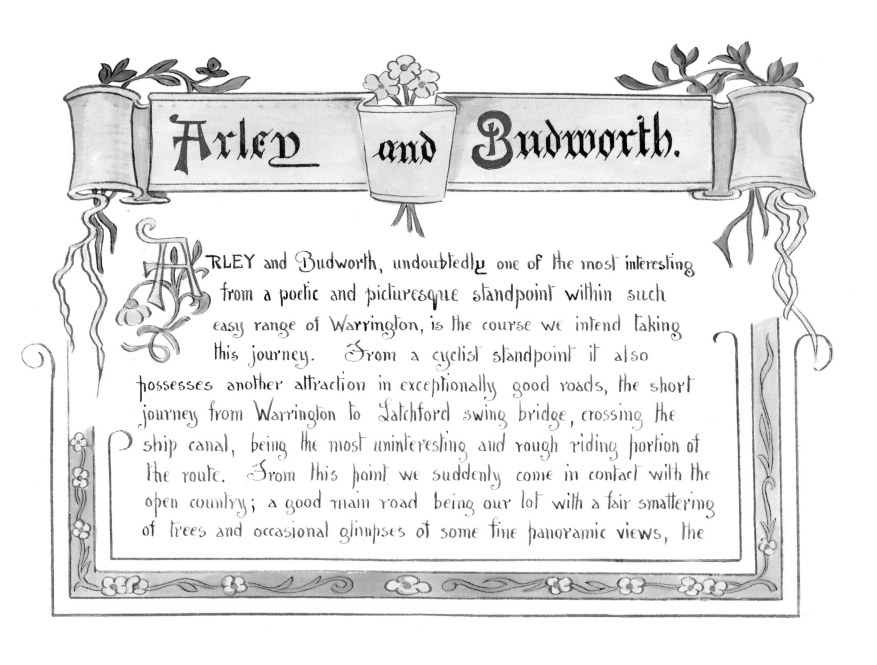

ARLEY and Budworth, undoubtedly one of the most interesting from a poetic and picturesque standpoint within such easy range of Warrington, is the course we intend taking this journey. From a cyclist standpoint it also possesses another attraction in exceptionally good roads, the short journey from Warrington to Latchford swing bridge, crossing the ship canal, being the most uninteresting and rough riding portion of the route. From this point we suddenly come in contact with the open country; a good main road being our lot with a fair smattering of trees and occasional glimpses of some fine panoramic views, the

GRAPPENHALL CHURCH.

first being Grappenhall, with its fine old red sandstone church nestling among the trees, surrounded
with picturesque whitewashed cottages. It being
but a short distance away it is well worth a —
flying visit, especially if you suffer from an —
artistic temperament and are afflicted with a
craving for a subject for a small sketch, but I
am afraid you would want more than a day
if you start out with the intention of sketching
all the suitable views on the route as they are
so numerous. Another subject a little further
on our road cannot but fail to attract,
though difficult to find if you are not acquainted
with the locality. I should say it would
be a little over a mile after passing under
the canal bridge on the Knutsford road,
you take a turn to the right along the first

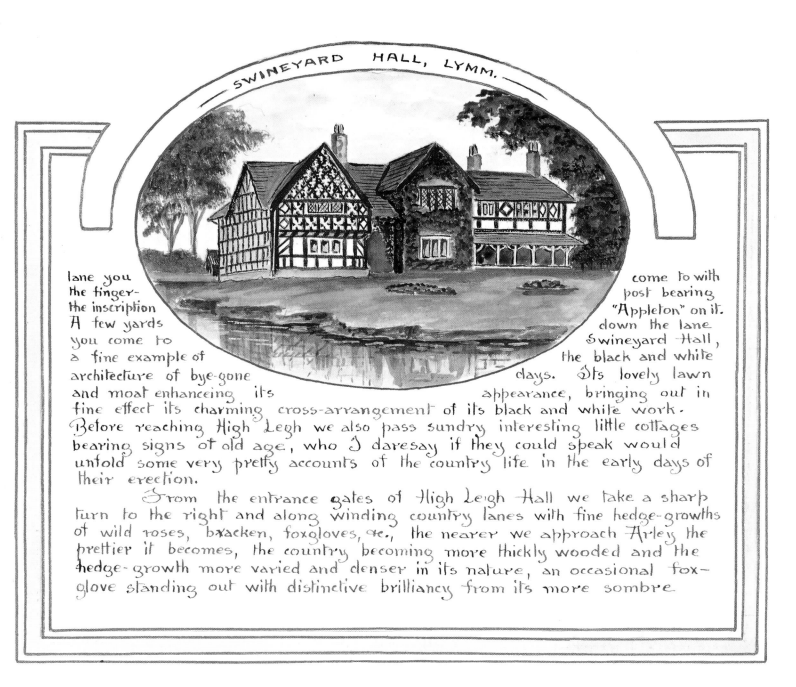

SWINEYARD HALL, LYMM.

lane you come to with the finger-post bearing the inscription "Appleton" on it. A few yards down the lane you come to Swineyard Hall, a fine example of the black and white architecture of bye-gone days. Its lovely lawn and moat enhanceing its appearance, bringing out in fine effect its charming cross-arrangement of its black and white work. Before reaching High Legh we also pass sundry interesting little cottages bearing signs of old age, who I daresay if they could speak would unfold some very pretty accounts of the country life in the early days of their erection.

From the entrance gates of High Legh Hall we take a sharp turn to the right and along winding country lanes with fine hedge-growths of wild roses, bracken, foxgloves, &c., the nearer we approach Arley the prettier it becomes, the country becoming more thickly wooded and the hedge-growth more varied and denser in its nature, an occasional fox-glove standing out with distinctive brilliancy from its more sombre surroundings, the winding narrow lanes with their abundance of dog-roses, honeysuckle, crab-apple blossom and a groundwork of bracken, meadowsweet, buttercups, wild pansy, bramble, celandine, &c. Ultimately we arrive at one of the celebrated poetic sign-posts, bearing the following rhyme :—

"This road forbidden is to all,
Unless they wend their way to call
At Mill or Green or Arley Hall."

In Arley and its vicinity there are a number of these poetic signs, composed by Mr. E. Egerton-Warburton. The Warburtons of Arley are one of the oldest Cheshire families, Mr. E. Egerton-Warburton, the composer of the rhyming signposts was born in 1804, a tipical country squire and model landlord, with a passion for literature and gained popularity in the district as a poet, most notable of which being the following hunting songs:— "The Little Red Rover," "Tantivy Trot," "Hard Riding Dick"; "Farmer Oldstyle"; also "Simple Sermons for Country Cottagers," "A Looking Glass for Landlords," and other homely poems.

THE VILLAGE SCHOOL

Towards the latter years of his life he became blind, and in his latest volume of verse, "Arley in Darkness," there are some touching references to his affliction. Our course takes us through an avenue of trees to Arley Pool, a most picturesque sheet of water lending itself at every conceivable point to the artist or camera fiend, who is desirous of obtaining a picture, the first being the mill, which can be sketched from three or four different standpoints with effect. It is small wonder that Mr. E. Egerton-Warburton was a poet when surrounded with such pretty scenery as this Arcadia. Leaving the mill we wend our way along a winding well-wooded lane, catching occasional glimpses of the water through the trees, arriving eventually at Arley Green, on which is a fine old barn, converted by Mr. E. Egerton-Warburton into a school.

The beams supporting the roof spring from the ground, meeting under the ridge of the roof and span the entire width of the building. It was here on this green that the squire used to play the part of fine old English gentleman, reviving some of the old customs and sports. There are many other picturesque features on Arley green, the smithy, cottages, &c., vieing with the old school for distinction. Our course takes us along a field-path by the side of the mere, where glimpses can occasionaly be got of Arley Hall, the home of the Warburton's, which stands in a well-wooded park of 300 acres, and was built by the aforementioned poetic squire on the site of the old Hall of Warburtons, erected in the 15th century. The present erection was commenced in 1833, being finished in 1842. Eventually we reach a country lane, which

Arley Hall.

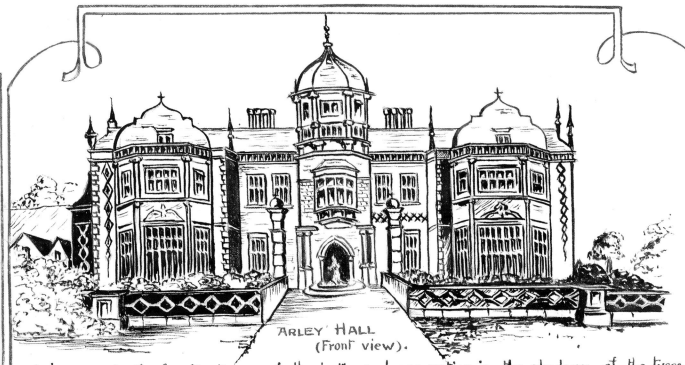

ARLEY HALL
(Front view).

brings us to the front entrance of the hall, and we notice in the shadows of the trees
to our right another of the poetic signs, vis:—

"No cartway, save on suffrance here,
For horse and foot the road is clear
To Lymm, High Legh, Hoo Green and Mere."

We keep straight ahead through an avenue of trees for a few yards till we
reach Arley post office, at which I am told some admirable photo postcards
can be obtained of the district. At the cottages in its vicinity refreshments can be
obtained, during which some valuable information re the hall and village are thrown
in gratis if you are so disposed to broach the topic to your host. Each of these

cottages are possessed of admirable gardens, whose blaze of color is a revelation after leaving the dark sombre shadows cast by the heavy foliage of the aforementioned trees.

We keep along the country lane and take the first turn to the left which takes us through a maze of country lanes of most varied styles of beauty, occasionally affording fine panoramic views, then densely wooded, then a charming effect of gorse bushes, bracken, wayside pools, cottages and more pretentious dwellings, eventually arriving at Budworth, the most ancient little village it has ever been my lot to come in contact with, taking our minds back to the times of Cromwell, with whom the church history is particularly associated. It is such places as Budworth that make England so attractive to the foreigner.

We are tempted to linger inside its church or in the "George and Dragon" on the opposite side of the road, within the porch of which there is written up a poetic admonition emanating from the pen of Mr. E. Egerton-Warburton to this effect:—

"As St. George in armed array
Doth the fiery Dragon slay
So mayest thou with might no less
Slay the Dragon Drunkenness."

GREAT BUDWORTH.

The village street claims particular attention from its irregularity and the quaintness of its architecture. Budworth standing well up on a hill commands some excellent views of the surrounding country Pickmere and Marbury Mere glistening like silver amid the green pasture lands and the thickly wooded Marbury Park. The latter mere being eight acres in extent and being so well-wooded and edged with rushes and underwood presents the most picturesque effect.

Descending the hill, at the bottom of which is the celebrated running pump, whose water is ascribed to have an healing property, and concerning which there are many traditions and poetic references, we come to a four-lane end and for preference we keep straight on although we could arrive at the same point by taking the turn to the left. Our course takes us along a pretty country lane with Marbury Mere to our left and cottage property (mostly thatched) and pastoral country to our right, passing through Comberbach and into a private road and on to as fine a specimen of large trees obtainable in the Northwich district, facing the entrance to Marbury Hall, the ancient home of the Barry family,

MARBURY HALL

who were descended from John, the youngest brother of the fifth earl of Barrymore. Two generations later this ancient family, which could carry its annals back to the Norman Conquest, became extinct in the person of Henry Barry, eighth earl of Barrymore. The hall is said to contain one of the most important private collections of works of art (painting and statuary) in the county as well as a large library. The collection was begun in 1771 by the Hon S. Smith-Barry. We proceed through the park to the land of salt, where evidences of the numerous subsidences are on every hand in the form of large sheets of water. If not seen before Northwich is worthy of a visit just to see the effect of the subsidencies by the sucking of the salt from below its surface, houses held together by iron girders, some with large cracks in them, toppling one into the other, and leaning in a dangerous manner over the side-walks, houses that once had steps up to the front doors having sunk to such a degree that the order has had to be reversed so that you have to descend instead of ascending the steps to reach the entrance. In fact if you have indulged freely in the liquors at the "George and Dragon" you would be apt to think the same has taken effect. I should its like would be unparrelled in any other mining district in the country. On our return journey through Marston, at the village church of which my wife and I were married, the unevenness of the property and the abundance of salt works begin to pall on us, and it is with relief that we again come in view of Budworth Church, standing in majestic splendor on the top of the hill, as though protecting its village from intruders, while on our left the waters of Marbury Mere edged with rushes and trees give the scene such a quiet, peaceful repose that by instinct we apply the break and slowly saunter along the country lane till we arrive once more at the running pump of Budworth. Since my previous reference to this pump I have paid the district another visit and obtained the legend respecting same. On close examination I also discovered a

THE RUNNING PUMP

tablet inside bearing the following inscription:—

"Blessings in never ending love   Springs from the bounteous earth below
Are on us poured from heaven above   Alike in both His goodness shown
This running stream with ceaseless flow   Whom heaven and earth their Maker own.

———— THE RUNNING PUMP. ————

A Legend of Big Budworth —— By the late R. E. Egerton-Warburton.

The village of Big Budworth! you may travel England round,
There is not such a village in the kingdom to be found,
It signifies in Saxon "By the water an abode."
And still that water floweth as in olden times it flow'd.

So pure, so bright, both day and night it bubbles and it flows,
The Running Pump they call it there, as everybody knows;
But, mind ye, 'tis the water that is running, not the pump—
'Tis all the pump can do to stand upon its rotten stump.

His sweetheart there the lover meets and tells her not to doubt
His love shall last so long as runs that water from the spout,
And there old crones together flock when summer evenings close,
And faster than the Running Pump the village gossip flows.

In every sky there is a cloud, however bright the morn,
In every sweet a bitter, in every rose a thorn:
So one fine day that fountain sweet sent forth a bitter smell,
Each lass who held her can there had to hold her nose as well.

How this befell tho' none can tell, yet one and all declare
Their thirst to quench with such a stench was more than they could bear
Each school miss wrote to tell mama their tea they could not take,
The more they fill the teapot, still the more their stomachs ache.

Of yore, if this had happen'd, they'd have sworn some wicked witch
Had dipp'd her broom and stirr'd it up with brimstone and with pitch:
That hag the doom of witchcraft had been fated to endure,
They'd have burnt her into ashes to effect a water cure.

Some laid the blame on Willett, he, who doctors all the town,
The physic, which his patients could not swallow, had pour'd down;
Some said it was a trick which Wright the publican had play'd,
That the water he had hocussed for the good of his own trade.

The master of the school he said it tasted of red ink:
Said Newhall, 'tis the overflow of cesspool or of sink:
John Lewis, when they told him, flatly said it was not true,
They went and told the Steward, but he only said "pooh! pooh."

The LEGEND OF THE RUNNING PUMP — continued.

They resolved to hold a Meeting, and they call'd it then and there;
Drinkwater was the proper man they said to take the chair;
They borrow'd paper, pen and ink, and straightway they began
To write a requisition to the Squire, and thus it ran :

"We, the undersign'd inhabitants of Budworth, Budworth Big,
Potatoes now we cannot boil, we cannot scald a pig ;
And those who send their milk away to Warrington for sale,
Have not a drop of water fit to teem into the pail."

"Should the Vicar bring an action you will have to pay the shot
If you stint us in cold water you will find yourself in hot;
This petition, its condition showeth plainly by the dirt
That we cannot wash our fingers, no—nor change our Sunday
shirt.

"The water, like the pump itself, quite rotten is and stale,
Of that bereft we've nothing left but George and Dragon ale:
We cannot mix our porridge with no water in the pot;
If we do not die of hunger we shall perish of dry rot."

"Our faith upon the Running Pump has hitherto been pinn'd
But how when short of water can we hope to raise the wind;
So Squire, unless we get redress, and pretty quickly too,
We, your tenants of Big Budworth, we will wash our hands of you.

Cooke, Dutton, Burgess, Barber, Summer, Bebbington and Platt,
All, young and old, their hands uphold and say "aye! aye!" to that
Then those who cannot write their names a cross upon it scrawl
And straight they went their document to carry to the Hall.

The Squire thought first the Fenians had from prison broke away,
He looked again and said "Good men what come ye here to say !
Has Rinderpest broke out afresh! is Budworth Church on fire!"
"Fire! not a bit! read what we've writ, 'tis water we require."

A notion as he read it, flash'd like lightning through his mind,
Or salt or sulphur it might be, or both of them combined :
"Though the gold mine prov'd a failure, though the nugget was no go,
Still gold into my pocket from the Running Pump may flow.

"I'll draw a plan, and spick and span build up a new hotel :
The world forsaking Harrogate, shall fly to Budworth well,
It may turn out a cure for gout, it may be full of steel,
Weak nerves to cure, which all endure, who call themselves genteel.

"Nay! who can tell, to try this well her majesty the Queen
May condescend to come and spend a summer at the Dene."
He bade his groom go saddle him a hunter of good-speed,
And straight, across the Arley Moss he prick'd his flying steed.

He reached the Pump—alas! when there he found himself at fault
It neither smelt of sulphur, neither tasted it of salt;
The wry face he made o'er it told the thing was past a joke,
That, sure enough, was not the stuff for fashionable folk.

He bade them dig, and spadeful upon spadeful they upcast,
And what do you think of all this stink the reason was at last;
A marvel then no longer how this strange thing came to pass
Some one there had been and gone and buried a dead ass.

Almost facing the pump is another poetic admonition inscribed on the front of a pretty cottage which you may possibly overlook as your attention may be detracted to its beautiful garden, viz:—

"Take thy calling thankfullie
Love thy neighbour neighborlie
Shun the path to beggarie."

We eventually arrive at the "Cock," which by the way we must not pass without some slight reference. It appears that about 250 years ago there passed through the village a character well-known as "Drunken Barnaby", who stopped for a day or two at the "Cock." Of this adventure Drunken Barnaby wrote the following:—

"Thence to the "Cock" at Budworth, where I
Drunk strong ale as brown as berry :
Till at last with deep health felled,
To my bed I was compelled ;
I for state was bravely sorted,
By two porters well supported.

Where no sooner understand I
Of mine honest host Tom Grandi,
To Holme-Chappell forthwith set I
Maid and Hostesse both were pretty,
But to drink took I affection,
I forgot soon their complexion

A poorly-painted picture may be seen at the "Cock" representing this Drunken Hero being carried off to bed by two men.

Resuming the saddle we pass through as fine a piece of roadside scenery as is obtainable in the Warrington districts, leafy dells, panoramic scenery, picturesque cottages with excellent gardens, then open pasture with mild-eyed cows blinking sleepily at one another, quiet little hamlets and farmsteads being the component parts of what could be dwelt on to considerable length had we the space to spare.

Arriving at Stretton Church, a fine old church and a notorious landmark, though to me it presents a rather lonely appearance. We take the turn to our left for preference, but before doing so I would like to draw attention to the "Cat and Lion" on the right with its poetic sign, representing a mild looking lion and a ferocious looking cat, around which is written :—

" The Lion is strong   My ales are good
  The Cat is vicious   And so are my liquors."

From Stretton Church to Pepper Street, Appleton Cross, is purely pastoral country. Pepper Street, by the way, resembles a country lane and is the only street of which this little hamlet can boast. Appleton Thorne is more pretentious, having a church, school, smithy a few cottages, and a small inn called the "Thorne" for which Mr. Egerton-Warburton composed the following:—

"As long as you're sober, you're safe at the Thorn,
But if drunk over night, it will prick you next morn;
May the lord of the manor who planted it thrive,
May the wenches who bawm it, all speedily wive,
May the old 'neath its shadows in comfort repose,
And Appleton flourish as long as it grows."

The two first lines may be seen inscribed over the door of the inn. At one time the village used to keep up the old custom of "barning the Thorn" (bawning the Thorn) on the 29th day of June, St. Peter's Day, when the school children in their white dresses and brilliantly coloured sashes danced and sang on the village green :—

"Barn the old thorn
At peep of dawn
This happy morn
Barn the Thorn."

We turn abruptly to the left at Appleton Church and are favoured with an excellent free-wheel along a country lane which affords fine panoramic views of Hill Warren and district, eventually arriving at the "Dingle," a favourite resort for Warringtonians, not so much on account of its nearness to Warrington, but principally owing to its natural ~~but~~ beauty, it being one of those pretty spots that adapt themselves to the seasons, in the spring for its freshness and delicacy of tints, summer for its heavy foliage and cooling shadows, autumn for its colour, and winter for its hoar-frosts, ultimately we arrive on the London-road, when our journey is practically ended as we are barely a mile from Stockton Heath. The least said about the road from Stockton Heath to Warrington the better, suffice it to say that from a cycling standpoint it is the worst bit of road I have ever ridden over.

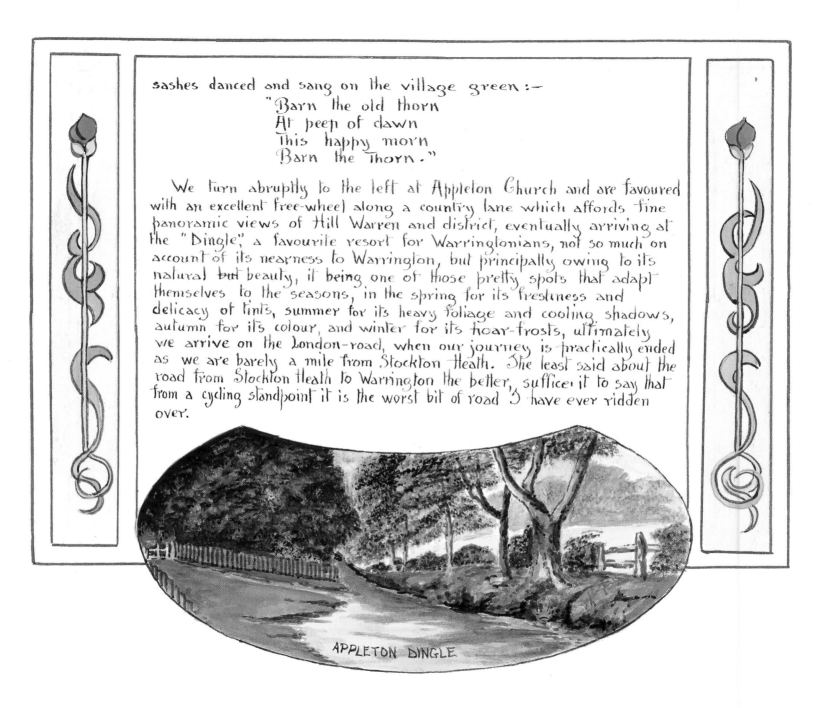

APPLETON DINGLE

Alderley Edge.

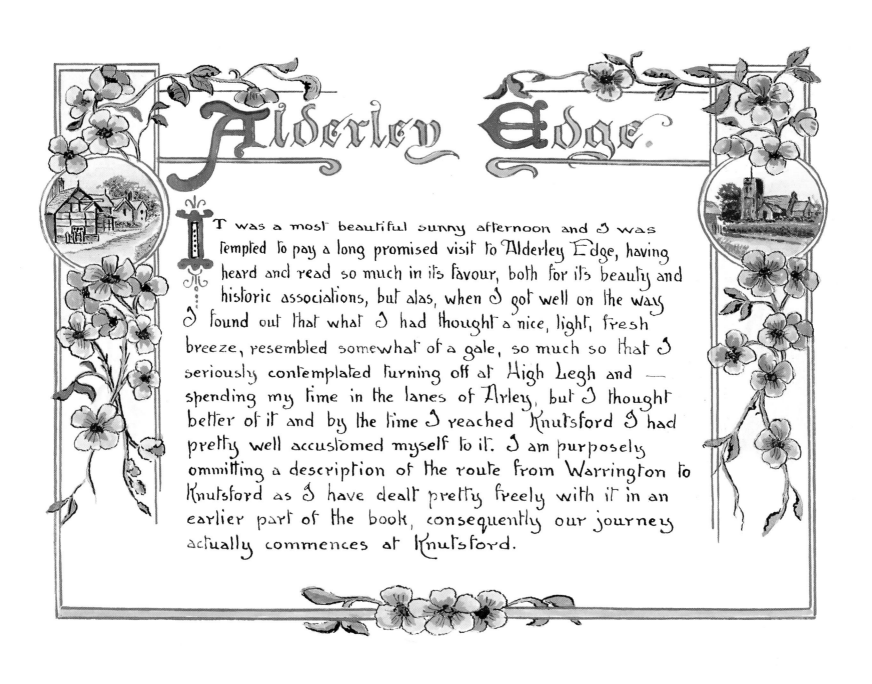

IT was a most beautiful sunny afternoon and I was tempted to pay a long promised visit to Alderley Edge, having heard and read so much in its favour, both for its beauty and historic associations, but alas, when I got well on the way I found out that what I had thought a nice, light, fresh breeze, resembled somewhat of a gale, so much so that I seriously contemplated turning off at High Legh and — spending my time in the lanes of Arley, but I thought better of it and by the time I reached Knutsford I had pretty well accustomed myself to it. I am purposely ommitting a description of the route from Warrington to Knutsford as I have dealt pretty freely with it in an earlier part of the book, consequently our journey actually commences at Knutsford.

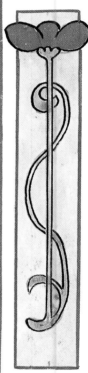

After leaving the Unitarian Chapel at Knutsford and climbing the hill on the Macclesfield Road I was brought into touch with some really picturesque highway scenery. It was an ideal road, well wooded on either side. About a mile out of Knutsford, situated on the side of the road stands a stone column, having a background of sombre foliage, giving it a most picturesque and imposing appearance. I tried to trace its history, but failed, and their is no inscription on it to indicate its purpose.

The next two miles was a journey on a good, hard macadam road with tall, stately chestnuts, birches, &c., on either side of the road, and where the road narrows I passed through a natural archway of foliage; then gradually the country became more open, though by no means lacking in detail, an occasional clump of trees, a cottage, an old mansion, with its pretty garden, a wayside pool, &c., all adding their attractions and breaking up the remotest sign of monotony. The better class of scenery really commenced at Chelford, when the road took more the resemblance of a country lane, excepting for the beautiful condition the road itself was kept in, which is a rarety in a country lane.

The first thing that struck me was the number of men in uniform with the metal initials M.A. on their arms; it afterwards dawned on me that they would be the motor scouts I had heard of but never previously seen. I was not long left in doubt as to their duties, which appeared to be that of point duty at various cross-roads and they were certainly needed as the motor traffic was terrible and to a great extent marred what would have otherwise been an ideal country lane with an abundance of wild roses and honeysuckle growing in the hedge-way.

From Monks Heath the road became wider, though it lost none of its beauty, the ride through Alderley Park being all that could be desired, tall, stately trees

NETHER ALDERLEY.

line the road, through which glimpses could be had of various meadows, and ancient dwellings and cottages, the whole having a dense background of trees. On reaching Nether Alderley the scene took a change, emerging from the dense foliage of the park we are confronted with an ancient little hamlet comprising half-timbered, thatched and old-fashioned, cottages, an old corn mill, and a cross, with a fair quantity of foliage to relieve same. The cross, situated on our left, at the corner of Welsh Row is particularly striking, standing as it does in front of a white farmhouse with diamond-paned windows, the cross itself being almost hidden by the foliage of a gnarled and twisted thorn, which seems as old as he very stones from which it appears to have taken root, alongside of which is a four-armed finger-post, while on the opposite side of the road is an inevetable horsepond, while looking down the lane we catch sight

CROSS OF NETHER ALDERLEY.

of old-fashioned thatched cottages. On our right we have the old mill and Artists' Lane, and if you have a camera or pencil you will be in a dilemma which to copy first. In a local guide I came across the following, which I think appropriately describes it, viz:—

"The ancient cross, itself scarce seen,
So shaded by a hawthorn green;
And near it still an old friend stands,
And guides our way with outstretched hands
Time-worn are both— but what their age
No record tells, nor village sage.

To our right we have the rectory, half buried in trees, situated in a beautiful old-world garden which runs right up to the church-yard and is almost overshadowed by the church, whose old walls and ~~gardens~~ tower is nearly overgrown with ivy. It has a projecting porch, with seats inside, and a round arch at the entrance. In the churchyard are some very old yew trees, the trunk of the one nearest the gate being something like 17 feet in circumference. The ancient font of the church was accidently discovered many years ago, buried in the ground and was placed in the churchyard, and is estimated to be somewhere about 600 years old. I must not omitt the ancient

ALDERLEY CHURCH.

sundial near the porch which helps to make the picture more perfect. Alderley village is a peculiar mixture of ancient and modern, though in all spotlessly clean and smart, having as a background the notorious mass of verdue clothed sandstone rock, standing 500 feet above the sea level, and 350 feet above the Cheshire plane, which stretches like a lovely carpet all round, it is irregular, crescent-shaped and extends over two miles of country. It is thickly wooded and has a beautiful undergrowth of hether, bracken, moss, lichen, grass, creepers, &c. I noticed that the fir tree was in evidence at almost every turn. The summit can be

OLD COTTAGES.
WELSH ROW, ALDERLEY

SOSSMOSS HALL   ALDERLEY

reached from various standpoints and after you have left the red-roofed, pretentious dwellings at base of the hill you could almost imagine you were climbing the Welsh mountains. From its summit some admirable views can be obtained of the Flintshire hills, Beeston Castle, and the surrounding country for miles. Some say that that beautiful watering place on the River Mersey, Runcorn and also Warrington can be seen, and even that pivot of commerce so noted for its pills, St. Helens, can be seen on a clear day. For a description of the places seen from Stormy Point we would need another book as they are so numerous, especially if you have sampled the liquors of the celebrated "Wizard," a picturesque inn on the summit of the Edge, but I am forgetting it has lately had its licence taken off it by Lord Sheffield, though it is still a place of refreshment for man and beast, but without the licence it has held for over 200 years. There is a legend which runs that the spot on which the "Wizard" now stands was under the spell of a powerful wizard from which the inn has derived its name. The story runs:- a Mobberley farmer, the owner of a fine white horse, famous in the district for its glossy coat was wending his way to a fair at Macclesfield to dispose of same. As he rode over the lonely hills of Alderley he was suddenly confronted by

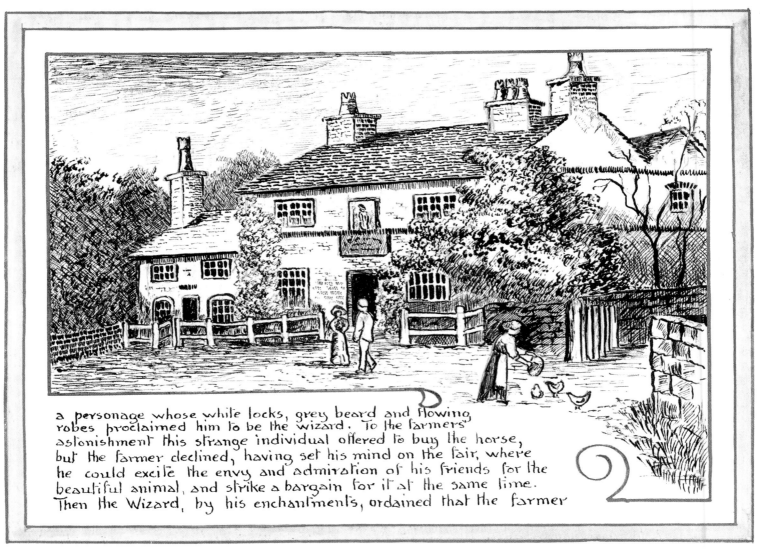

a personage whose white locks, grey beard and flowing
robes proclaimed him to be the wizard. To the farmers'
astonishment this strange individual offered to buy the horse,
but the farmer declined, having set his mind on the fair, where
he could excite the envy and admiration of his friends for the
beautiful animal, and strike a bargain for it at the same time.
Then the Wizard, by his enchantments, ordained that the farmer

should not find a purchaser, and he was obliged to return home with his horse unsold. On reaching the Wizard's cave he was again confronted by the Wizard and this time agreed to sell the horse. The Wizard waved his wand, when a voice like thunder was heard. Suddenly the hillside was cleft asunder, and across the yawning gulf the terrified farmer beheld a pair of huge gates. At a word from the Wizard the mighty barrier swung back, and the farmer, conducted by his wierd companion, led his horse into a deep cavern, whose vast extent was lost in the blackness of night. On and on went the Wizard, followed by the farmer, until at last they reached a cave where hundreds of white horses, with men clad in armour, were resting. One of the stalls was, however, empty, and into this the farmer was commanded to lead his horse. The Wizard expressed his satisfaction that the horse of the farmer completed the number he required, and he directed the farmer to help himself from a pile of gold and rare jewels which he displayed to his view. The farmer, it is said, had no scruples on this score, and loaded himself with gold and precious stones. At a signal from the Wizard the caverns, horses and horsemen disappeared, and the farmer, on recovering from his amazement, found himself on the road again. He made the best of his way to Mobberley, where the story of his adventure excited great wonder. The mythical tale further states that the army of the Wizard rests in the cave until the time when they shall awake from their enchanted sleep and sweep down upon their foes in the Cheshire plain, and decide the fate of England in a great battle.

OLD HALL, ALDERLEY

The "Wizard" Inn is an ancient, unpretentious, white-washed hostelry, and is surrounded by pinewoods, lending itself in a most delightful manner to pen or camera. We are also in close proximity to the Beacon, an historic erection, which recalls the warlike and stormy times of our ancestors. There is one important feature I should have mentioned earlier on, viz:— the old hall, Alderley. Little remains worthy of

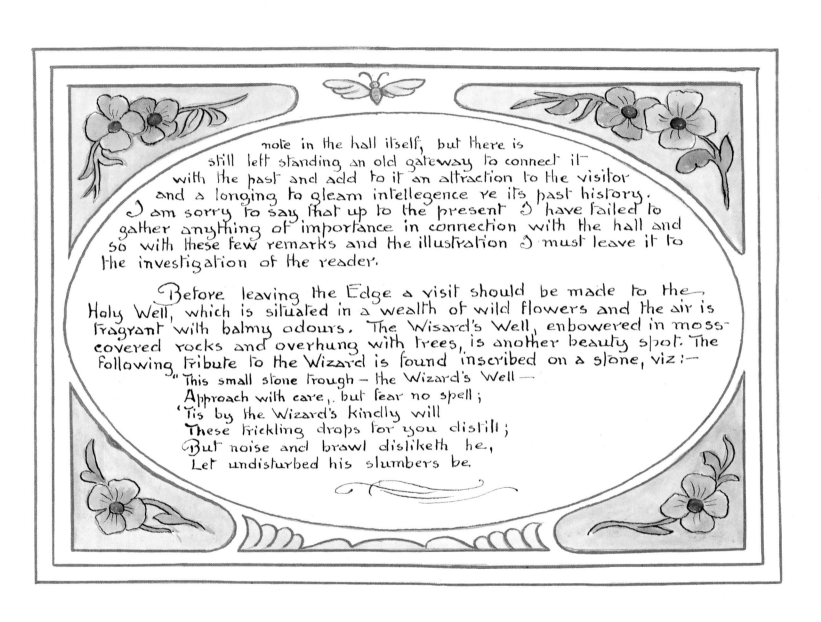

note in the hall itself, but there is
still left standing an old gateway to connect it
with the past and add to it an attraction to the visitor
and a longing to gleam intellegence re its past history.
I am sorry to say that up to the present I have failed to
gather anything of importance in connection with the hall and
so with these few remarks and the illustration I must leave it to
the investigation of the reader.

Before leaving the Edge a visit should be made to the
Holy Well, which is situated in a wealth of wild flowers and the air is
fragrant with balmy odours. The Wizard's Well, enbowered in moss-
covered rocks and overhung with trees, is another beauty spot. The
following tribute to the Wizard is found inscribed on a stone, viz:—
"This small stone trough — the Wizard's Well —
Approach with care, but fear no spell;
'Tis by the Wizard's kindly will
These trickling drops for you distill;
But noise and brawl disliketh he,
Let undisturbed his slumbers be.

HAWTHORNE HALL WILMSLOW.

Leaving Alderley we cross the railway bridge and on to
Wimslow, which I must confess is rather tame after the beauties
of Alderley Edge, although by no means lacking in interest, the church, standing
on rather low lying land, with the river Bollin glistening like a silver serphent,
and the irregular groups of cottage property all having their attractions.
Hawthorne Hall, about half a mile from the church is particularly pretty.
It is a many gabled building of comparatively modern erection, built by

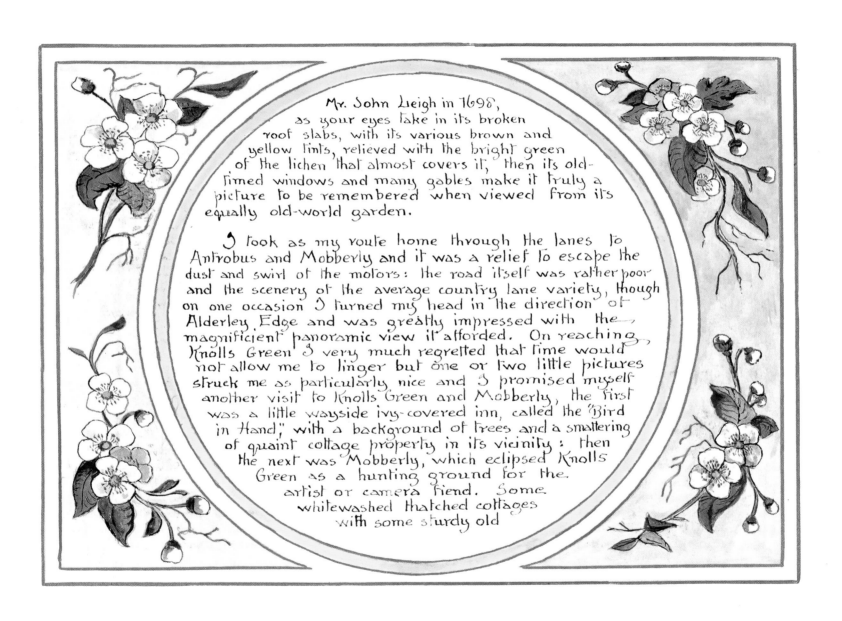

Mr. John Leigh in 1698,
as your eyes take in its broken
roof slabs, with its various brown and
yellow tints, relieved with the bright green
of the lichen that almost covers it, then its old-
timed windows and many gables make it truly a
picture to be remembered when viewed from its
equally old-world garden.

I took as my route home through the lanes to
Antrobus and Mobberly and it was a relief to escape the
dust and swirl of the motors: the road itself was rather poor
and the scenery of the average country lane variety, though
on one occasion I turned my head in the direction of
Alderley Edge and was greatly impressed with the
magnificent panoramic view it afforded. On reaching
Knolls Green I very much regretted that time would
not allow me to linger but one or two little pictures
struck me as particularly nice and I promised myself
another visit to Knolls Green and Mobberly, the first
was a little wayside ivy-covered inn, called the "Bird
in Hand," with a background of trees and a smattering
of quaint cottage property in its vicinity: then
the next was Mobberly, which eclipsed Knolls
Green as a hunting ground for the
artist or camera fiend. Some
whitewashed thatched cottages
with some sturdy old

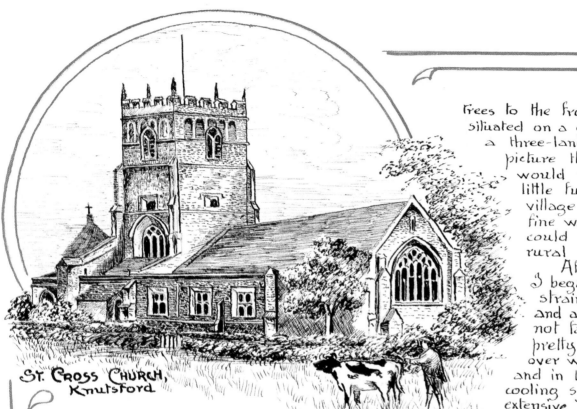

ST. CROSS CHURCH,
Knutsford

Trees to the front of them, situated on a grassy bank at a three-lane end was a picture that any artist would revel in, then a little further on by the village post office some fine water-colour sketches could be obtained of rural life.

After leaving Mobberly I began to feel the strain of the long ride, and although I could not fail to admire the pretty country lanes over which I travelled and in the distance the cooling shades of the extensive Tatton Park, I was by no means sorry when I came in view of the square tower of St. Cross Church, the roofs of houses and the spirey roofs of Knutsford gaol. On passing through the town I was almost tempted to stop and have some light refreshment, but second thoughts prevailed and I proceeded along Heath Lane to Rostherne, Buckley Hill, Lymm, and home. Having dealt previously with the above-mentioned places there is no necessity to go into details and had I felt so disposed I am afraid I would not have been able to give a very glowing account of same as I was too wearied with my exertions to take anything but the barest possible interest in my surroundings, and smoky old Warrington was as beautiful as Venice or Naples to me when I arrived there.

CHESTER.

It was the first Saturday in September and a glorious afternoon when I left home for an afternoon's spin with no definite destination with the exception of getting somewhere in the vicinity of Delemere Forest. The roads from Warrington to Cuddington were in excellent condition but nothing very striking from a scenic standpoint, though fairly pretty in places, consequently I had an opportunity to resolve on a destination, which resulted in Chester via the forest. I liked Cuddington: it being one of those pretty, clean and neat little villages that associate themselves with the city man's ideal of rural serenity. From Cuddington to Norley was undoubtedly pretty and interesting country but I had to confess to a feeling of dissapointment at not coming in contact with the notorious forest. It was not till reaching the Abbey Arms that my wishes were gratified as I seemed to suddenly come to the fringe of the forest. For about half a mile it was positively fascinating, leafy dells, woodland paths through bracken and underwood, giving the incentive to numerable

DELAMERE

TARVIN

DUNHAM HILL

FRODSHAM

imaginary pictures of a forest of immense dimensions, but alas we come to a clearing and we realise that the forest is no more. In 1850 it covered something like 8,000 acres, whereas now it can only boast of about 4,000 acres and most of that cut up. Only remnants of its past grandeur in the patches of woodland here and there being all that remains. We have to discard the idea of forest land and take the country as it is:- pretty and well-wooded, the effect being greatly enhanced by the abundance of fir trees standing out in sombre relief against the lighter green foliage of the other trees. The country is also hilly and consequently lends an added charm to the scene.

After passing through the village of Kelsall, which seems to open itself out as a catering centre for visitors, the road seems to take us more into these woods, the density of which is particularily striking to the left. The whole scene taking us back to early days

when deer abounded in the woods, which for some unaccountable reason Charles I. ordered to be destroyed. It was at this point that I realised that I was riding on the outside fringe instead of through the heart of the forest that had once been Cheshire's glory, but I was compensated by the panoramic views to my right and thickly wooded hillsides to my left with occasionally an apparent invasion of the road into the forest, and slumbering little hamlets and above all the rich and glorious hedgegrowth. I was pleased that I had chosen this course if only for the pleasure of seeing the quaint old village of Tarvin with its old red sandstone church nestling in the midst of equally quaint dwellings: an irregular street with a pitable attempt at modinization in the form of scraggy trees with iron railings round them. I would not have been surprised to have seen huntsmen, with their brilliantly red coats, clattering through the streets with a pack of hounds following Although averse to hunting or any form of sport that means suffering and pain to animals of lower stage than ourselves, I have to admit that these red-coated hunters lend the one touch of color and animation to the drab of these sleepy old streets villages that seem to be needed to make the scene complete. After leaving Tarvin we notice a most marked change in the landscape, the road looses its switchback nature and the country its thickly wooded appearance. Pasture-land is more in evidence and by we arrive at Stamford Bridge it has positively evolved itself into a flat swampy country with a class of beauty which is equally as

fascinating as that we have already passed through. Its very openness is apt to inspire one to indulge in deep breathing exercises, which we unconsiously find ourselves doing, the very grass seems to have taken a lease of life, retaining its vivid emerald green appearance, the flocks of sheep and herds of cows only making it look more vivid and also adding scenic effect. From Stamford Bridge this is particularly noticeable and numerable water-color sketches could be obtained from the district which I guarantee would be more fresh and crisp than any the same artist could paint of the forest and its surroundings. From here to Chester is an excellent road, and three miles out of Chester we ride through a particularly pretty avenue of trees for about a mile or so till we ultimately arrive at the class of building that are invariably to be found outside a city; uninteresting on the whole, but gradually as we approach the city we feel that we are entering into a place of untold interest to the historian, antiquarian, author, artist, or any lover of the antique.

In the year 60 Chester was a Roman military station and was called "Deva" (the city on the Dee). Since that period it has passed through most stirring scenes. In 607 it was sacked by Ethelred and captured in 830 by Egbert. The Danes destroyed the city in 894, but it was restored by Ethelred, King of Mercia. At the time of the Norman conquest Chester was granted as a County Palatine to Hugh Lupus, who was at liberty to increase his territory by raids upon the Welsh. In 1156 Henry II came to the city with his troops and encamped at Saltney. Until 1237 the Earl Palatine maintained rule but Henry III attached the earldom to the Crown and the Prince of Wales received the title of the Earl of Chester. War, riots, and plagues seem to have been the lot of early Chester of which lengthy accounts can be obtained from most books in public libraries dealing with the early history of the north of England.

It is practically impossible to go into any detail of Chester and its attractions without touching on its historic association as it is in that that its glory lay, but I shall curtail my description as much as possible and shall deal with what I consider its chief attractions.

I think the best thing to do is to start by traversing the walls, which boast a circumference of about two miles, being penetrated by a number of gateways. Parts of the north and east walls are of Roman construction, the remaining portion being mainly of Edwardian date, though work of the 13th and 15th century can also be traced. I think it is most advisable to commence the inspection at Eastgate, which was erected in 1769, by the Lord Governor of the period. Ascending the wall on the north of this gate and walk towards the Cathedral, of which an exceptionally fine view is obtainable, and on to the next gate which stands at the end of Abbey Street, being known as Kale-yard gate. This gate, which is only a postern, and much smaller than the main entrances to the city, was made for the convenience of monks when visiting their kitchen or kale-garden, a spot now covered by a school and a timber-yard. Next we come to Newton's Tower, better known as Phœnix Tower, the tower from which King Charles I, in the year 1646, watched the defeat of his troops on Rowton Moor. It is now converted into a museum and well worthy of a visit. At this point the wall takes us alongside the canal which is crossed by two bridges. The canal was cut in 1771, and was intended as a means of communication between Nantwich and Chester. It was the cutting of this canal which necessitated the building of the two bridges, the smaller of which being known as the "Bridge of Death" or "The Bridge of Sighs", and was built as a connection between Northgate and the Chapel of the Hospital of St. John, over which condemned prisoners passed from their last attendance upon a religious service to the place of their execution. The purpose of the bridge came to an end in 1708, when the city gaol near the infirmary came into use. We next come to "Morgan's Mount" from the upper platform of which a fine view is obtained of the Welsh mountains,

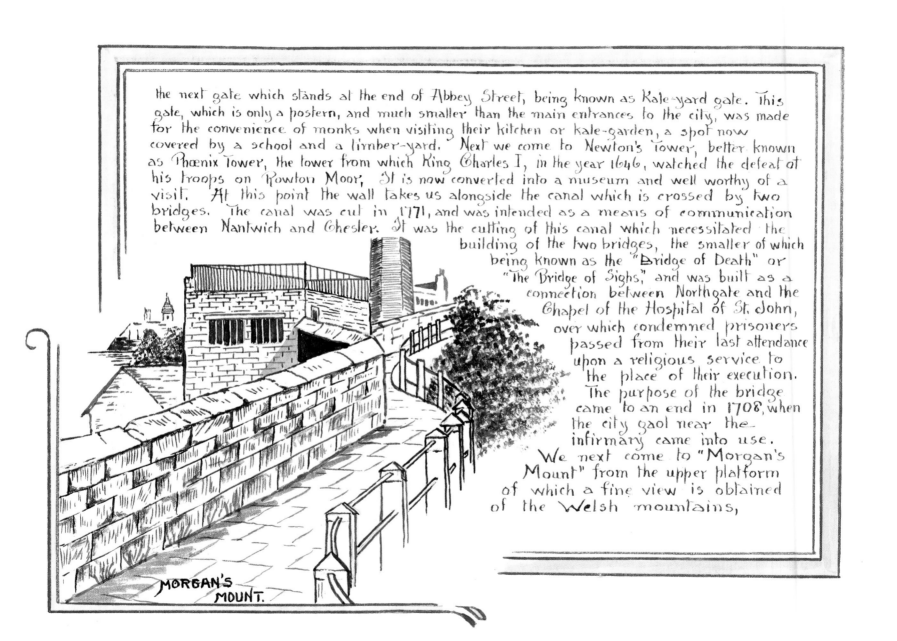

MORGAN'S MOUNT.

The Phoenix Tower.
"King Charles Tower."

The Water Tower.
Welsh hills in the distance.

after which comes Pemberton's Parlour, named after one John Pemberton, a rope-maker, who in 1700 established a ropewalk within the walls and is supposed to have sat in this tower — watching his men work below. In 1720 it underwent several repairs owing to its ruinous condition and has practically been rebuilt since that date. We next come to two towers, the highest of which is called "Bonewaldesthorne's" Tower, the smaller being called "New" or "Water" Tower, which in spite of its first name was originally built in the reign of Edw. II. When it was built the waters of the Dee came up to the walls at this point, and there were iron rings attached to the tower for the mooring of boats. We then skirt the Roodee, where the races are held, then we come in sight of the Benedictine nunnery of S. Mary on our left. It is now traversed by a road connecting Northgate with Grosvenor-road. This last named thoroughfare cuts through the walls before the Castle is reached, and crosses the river by a handsome stone bridge of one span, known as Grosvenor Bridge. We next pass the Castle on our left and the river and suburb of Handbridge on the right. The Castle now a military depot,

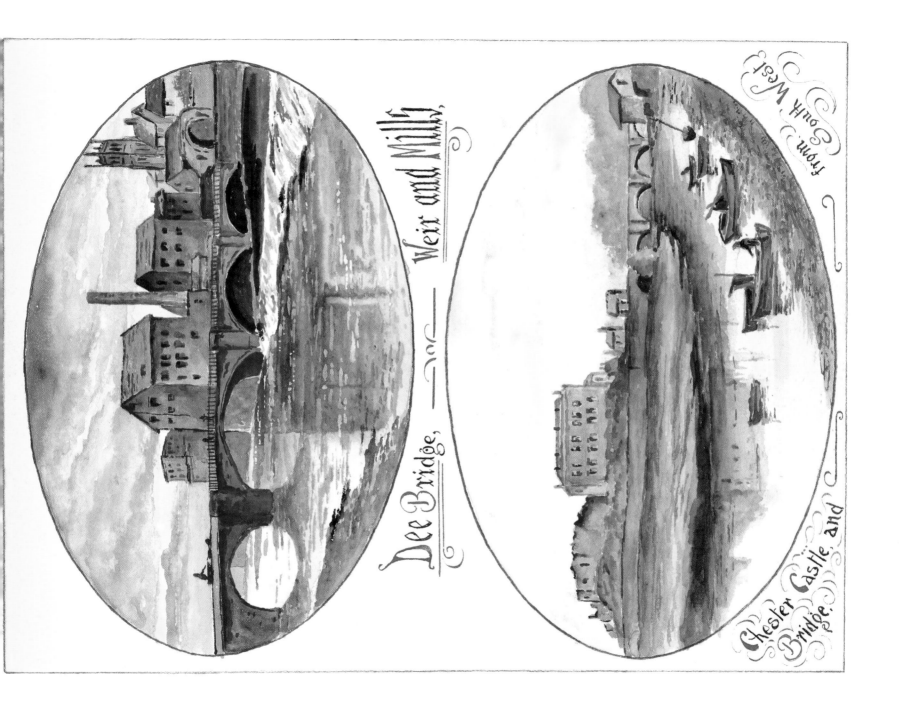

Dee Bridge, — Weir and Mills.

Chester Castle, and Bridge. — from South West.

stands on the site of what had apparently been an old Roman fortress and the present erection appears to have been built piece-meal. We next come to the Bridge and Mills. The Bridge stands on the site of at least three other bridges, one that was built in 1227, another in 1297, and one in 1353, all of which were washed away by floods, there is also mention of a wooden structure in the Doomesday Book. The bridge at present consists of seven arches, though it is supposed to have possessed a greater number. at one time. In 1826 a projecting footpath, seven feet in width, was added' to the structure.

The Mills, mention of which is made in the years 1351 and 1442, when it appears all people in Chester and vicinity were compelled to bring their corn to be ground in these mills, which meant a tremendous income to the Earls of Chester, to whom the mills belonged. They have three times been destroyed by fire, but the present buildings occupy the identical spot on which mills were erected at least as somewhere about the end of the eleventh century.

We now come to the "Wishing Steps." Folk-lore proclaims that if a person forms a wish and immediately after doing so runs from bottom to top, down again and once more up, without taking breath during the process, the wish

Wishing Steps.

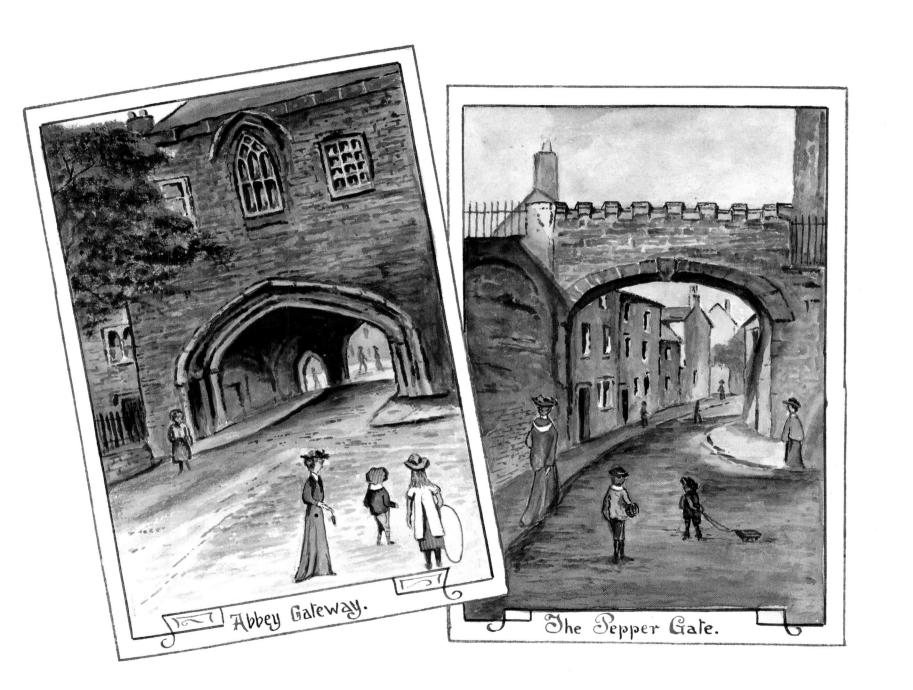

Abbey Gateway.

The Pepper Gate.

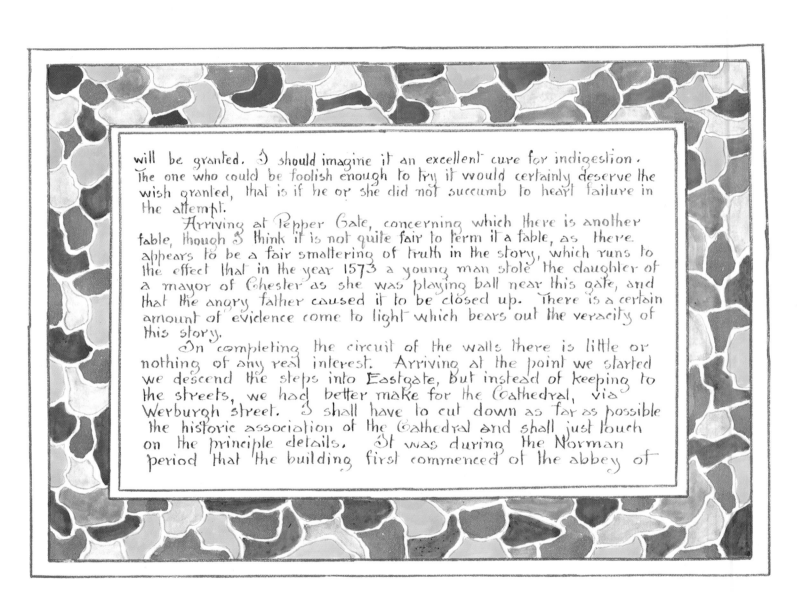

will be granted. I should imagine it an excellent cure for indigestion. The one who could be foolish enough to try it would certainly deserve the wish granted, that is if he or she did not succumb to heart failure in the attempt.

Arriving at Pepper Gate, concerning which there is another fable, though I think it is not quite fair to term it a fable, as there appears to be a fair smattering of truth in the story, which runs to the effect that in the year 1573 a young man stole the daughter of a mayor of Chester as she was playing ball near this gate, and that the angry father caused it to be closed up. There is a certain amount of evidence come to light which bears out the veracity of this story.

In completing the circuit of the walls there is little or nothing of any real interest. Arriving at the point we started we descend the steps into Eastgate, but instead of keeping to the streets, we had better make for the Cathedral, via Werburgh street. I shall have to cut down as far as possible the historic association of the Cathedral and shall just touch on the principle details. It was during the Norman period that the building first commenced of the abbey of

The Cathedral ---
from North-East.

The Cathedral ---
from Werburgh's Street

St. Werburgh on the site of what is supposed to have an old druidical temple: very little indeed remains to denote old age in the external architecture of the cathedral, but for one who delights in early English, Saxon and Norman architecture the inside of the Cathedral will be a perfect treasure trove, the Norman arches especially cannot fail to fascinate. The fine examples of wood-carving (both ancient and modern) in the Choir Stalls are exceptionally fine and worthy of a more detailed account, but the difficulty would be that if you started you would not know where to leave off, so we will pass on to the shrine of St. Werburgh, situated at the west end of the Lady Chapel. Up to recent years a large portion of this shrine formed part of the Bishop's Throne, but on the erection of the present wooden throne, the fragments found here and elsewhere were pierced together, the deficiencies being made good with perfectly plain pieces of stone, so that all that remains of the old work can easily be identified. It is in traversing the Cloisters that our thoughts are apt to wander back to the early days of the abbey of St. Werburgh, when the monks used same for study, recreation, etc., Along the north wall of the cloisters we come to a passage leading to the refectory, only half of which now remains. It is now used as a place for choir practices. You cannot fail to notice the pulpit with stairs leading up to it, one of the finest examples of early English architecture, from which the lector read passages from the Scriptures. The lower parts of the arches were no

St. Werburgh's Shrine
Chester Cathedral.

Lectern in the
Refectory.

ST. JOHN'S CHURCH.

(INTERIOR).

doubt formerly occupied by stone book-rests to support the heavy volumes from which he read,

While dealing with places of worship it would perhaps be as well if we paid a flying visit to St. John's Church, situate near Pepper Gate and the Bishop's Palace. It is of Saxon origin, probably dating from the time of Ethelred, King of Mercia, for Saxon crosses and coins have been found in the old foundations. The exterior is not impressive but the arches of the nave and aisles are Norman. During its career it suffered considerably by falls of its masonry. The centre tower fell in 1468 and again in 1572. In 1574 the north-west tower fell and was rebuilt, but fell again in 1881. The most interesting portion of the exterior is that which is in ruins, concerning which there are some very interesting accounts (see local guide books).

The Cloister Garth.

NORTH-EAST CORNER.

Ruins of St. John's Church.

EAST END.

After traversing the walls and inspecting the interior of the Cathedral and St John's Church you may feel disposed to refresh the inner man and if you wish to combine your refreshments with the antique there are some fine old inns at which refreshments may be obtained. There is the "Bear and Billet," in Lower Bridge, at one time the mansion of the Earls of Shrewsbury, who held a moiety of the sergeantry of the Bridge—gate, which they purchased in 1666. The house appears to have been erected in 1664, and is a fine, comparatively little restored example of black and white work. Then there is the "Yacht," the "Falcon" in Bridge Street, and several others too numerous to mention. The "Falcon" is exceptionally interesting for its elaborate design. I have never dined at these places myself as I prefer the more modern restaurant, though I have to confess to having discovered some very ancient relics, not recorded in history, in these places. Probably the author of that pathetic ballad "The Cock must have crowed when they built the Tower of Babel," partook of his lunch in one of these restaurants, that being the only reference to antiquity in this direction that could apply to Chester.

After refreshments you start with renewed vigor on your tour of inspection but it is advisable to confine your ~~search~~ research on externals as you would need a week if you were to investigate into every ancient fabric you came in contact with. The principle items of interest are the rows or galleries in Eastgate Street,

Half-timbered Houses.

The "Bear and Buffet" Shrewsbury House.

Whitefriars.

Watergate Street and Bridge Street. Some think they are of direct Roman porticoe descent but this is hardly fesible in face of the ruinous condition in which they left the city. George Borrow held the theory that these rows, to which you ascend by stairs up narrow passages, were originally built for the security of wares of the principal merchants against the Welsh. While we are in Watergate Street there are two places of interest that we cannot pass without reference.

The first is the "Stanley Palace", in a small court off Watergate Street, bearing the date 1591. It is a black and white architecture with three gables, one of the rooms of which is supposed to have been occupied by King Charles I on several occasions. Then there is "God's Providence House," also in Watergate Street, which attracts considerable interest to visitors. The present building was erected

STANLEY PALACE.

"GOD'S PROVIDENCE HOUSE"

in 1862, containing particles of the older erection of 1652. On one of the beams under the principle window is the following inscription:—"God's Providence is mine inheritance." The story runs that the inscription was put up because this house was the only one spared by the plague, which is rather strange considering the plague occurred five years' before its erection.

There are some fine examples of old architecture in various parts of the city: one especially interesting from a picturesque and antiquarian standpoing being in Whitefriars.

Before leaving the city there is one other old piece of architecture I should like to refer to, vis:— The Abbey Gateway, undoubledly one of the oldest entrances into the city. I think I have previously referred to it but in doing so ommitted to mention one rather sad, but interesting, item in connection with same. In a chamber over the gate was the place of confinement of one George Marsh, who was burnt at Chester for heresy.

The return home from Chester via Mickle Trafford is not quite as interesting as the outward journey, the initial stages being through mostly residential districts, beautiful houses and gardens, but not quite up to the standard of those we came in contact with in entering the city. From Trafford to Dunham was practically a repetition of a similar class of scenery we met with at Stamford Bridge, fresh open country with no striking detail with the exception of its pure open freshness. From Dunham Hill to Helsby we pass through very pretty thickly wooded lanes, especially to our right. On entering Helsby I had to confess to a feeling of disappointment. After seeing Chester with its picturesque buildings the modern red-bricked houses of Helsby jarred on my nerves, and had it not been for the rocky face of Helsby hill on the right I should have felt inclined to resent the village as an intrusion on my reflections of Chester. From Helsby to Frodsham there was a decided improvement in the landscape, the hills to our right gradually becoming more thickly wooded. A mile out of Frodsham we are confronted with the prettiest part of the journey home, the hills being thickly wooded presents a varied assortment of tints in green with the heather-covered hill of Frodsham standing out with distinctive prominence in the background. On our left we have the marshy meadows through which the river Mersey flows looking in the sunlight like a silver serpent. The village of Frodsham is a great improvement on that of Helsby, in fact so much so that I intend devoting an article on Frodsham, its hill, and part of the forest. On that account I shall make very little

reference to the village or
the intervening districts between
here and Warrington, suffice it to say
that it is a good road and we pass through
one or two interesting places of which we will
have to refer anon. Daresbury especially I
should like to deal with, but shall reserve same for
a future occasion.

By the time I had arrived at Warrington I was
completely fagged out, and I should not advise anyone
who is not an expert cyclist to take the route I took
as it is by a long way too far for one journey:— the
outward journey to Chester being 25½ miles, and
the return journey 20 miles, making 45½ miles altogether.

THE END.

HENRY JOSIAH ATTY

Henry Josiah Atty was born in 1874 in Newton in Makerfield, Lancashire, and arrived in Warrington penniless sometime before the end of the century. Initially he worked as a compositor but later was able to open his own print shop, trading as a general and commercial printer and stationer.

He married Margaret Eccleston, a skilled seamstress, in 1900 and they lived in Warrington for the rest of their lives. They had no children of their own but were 'Uncle Harry' and 'Auntie Maggie' to many. Maggie became a spiritualist and regularly held seances in their home.

Henry Atty is remembered as a kind, quietly spoken, gentle man. Wearing a long overcoat, scarf and trilby, he would set out to draw local scenes, his sketchpad and pencils in a roll under his arm. Painting was his relaxation and, at home in the evening, he would work at his easel by gaslight, often painting on the sides of cardboard boxes. Financially, life was not easy.

Very generous with what he produced, he gave his pictures away as wedding presents, or simply as gifts, and continued to paint and draw for many years. He died in 1961. Fondly remembered by so many for his warmth and talent, Henry Atty was an artist not concerned with being more widely recognised but with the pleasure he brought to those around him.

Henry Atty, photograph taken in the 1940s.